Christ's Gifts to WOMEN

To our mothers, grandmothers, and all the women in our lives who have buoyed us up and left footsteps to follow; may we all find a sister to walk with as we seek to discover the Master and embrace His gifts.

We are greatly indebted to our early readers: Emily Halverson, Gayle Brown, and S. Kent Brown. Each provided insightful and indispensable editorial suggestions, and our gratitude is boundless. Continual thanks to Desiree Johns for her efficiency, late nights, and very keen eye. And as always, many thanks to the talented Covenant family for bringing this project to the community at large. We are grateful for your vision and camaraderie.

Quotes by Church leaders are used by permission. Intellectual Reserve, Inc.

Cover art: Mary Kept All Of These Things And Pondered Them In Her Heart © 2012 Howard Lyon - For print information go to www.fineart.howardlyon.com or call 480-241-7907

Cover design copyright © 2012 by Covenant Communications, Inc.
Cover and book design by Christina Marcano.

Published by Covenant Communications, Inc.
American Fork, Utah

Printed in China
First Printing: March 2012

19 18 17 16 15   10 9 8 7 6 5 4 3

ISBN-13: 978-1-60861-861-3

Christ's Gifts to WOMEN

HEATHER B. MOORE AND ANGELA ESCHLER

TABLE OF CONTENTS

INTRODUCTION

If thou knewest the gift of God . . .

—John 4:10

At Jacob's now-ancient well, an untutored daughter of God questions Jesus of Nazareth regarding the meaning of His words: what is this water He speaks of, and how is it possible to quench her thirst forever? Not even the great and honored patriarchs can boast of eliminating such needs. Because she does not yet understand who Jesus is or the power He holds, she cannot comprehend the gift He offers. Responding to her confusion, Christ says, "If thou knewest the gift of God, and who . . . [I am]; thou wouldest have asked . . . and [I] would have given thee living water" (John 4:10).

Many of us, as latter-day daughters of God, are equally bewildered regarding our relationship with our Elder Brother; we don't fully grasp who He is to us, our worth to Him, or the gifts He offered then and now. Considering the false, oppressive doctrines and pharisaic shepherds of Christ's day, we may see how ground-breaking His claim was regarding the worth of all souls, but do we recognize that it is just as revolutionary in our personal contexts today?

As we look at our sisters throughout history, we may easily understand, given the loud and belittling voices surrounding them and their being treated as second-class citizens or even as property, why many of Christ's daughters found it difficult to understand what He taught about their inherent worth—a worth so profound that He would die so that they could live, not only

Woman [shall] be recompensed in rich measure for all [she] . . . has endured in mortality. Then shall woman reign by Divine right, a queen in the resplendent realm of her glorified state.

eternally but each day more abundantly (see John 10:10). And as we look back on them and indentify how dangerous the world's lies were then and how they continue to endanger our souls now, we must find a way to embrace Christ's teachings and escape worldly messages unscathed. Many of us today too frequently struggle under the burdens of criticism, self-recrimination, fear, doubt, unnecessary and unproductive guilt, and even abuse. Such weight often becomes so heavy we feel we cannot bear it. To compound the problem, our spheres of influence and stewardship can appear as vast—and sometimes as impassible—as the seas that encompass the earth. Rather than seeing these responsibilities as a sign of Christ's bright faith in us, we see them as indicators of our limitations. Perhaps most distressing, we do not relinquish this load easily, and thus our ultimate power for good is greatly compromised.

It's not that we fail to rationally understand the doctrine of Christ, but we do struggle to see how those doctrines can be applied in our lives—how Christ's overcoming the world means even more than ultimate salvation after this life. While we strive to live up to our covenants, even with the blessings of the restored gospel at our fingertips, we are sometimes unable to find the daily peace Christ promises in return. As much as this enigma is troubling, it should not be surprising, for it is merely a fulfillment of prophecy. President Ezra Taft Benson promises that in the latter days, Satan will increasingly strive "to overcome the Saints with despair, discouragement, despondency, and depression."[1]

It is no wonder that this method of oppression is the favored strategy of the adversary; when he can "destroy [our] peace and afflict [our] soul" (2 Nephi 4:27), we cannot be the pillars of strength, example, and faith the Lord needs in these latter days.

Perhaps this is why the Lord's message was called the "good news"—the literal meaning of the word *gospel*.[2] Christ's good news is simply this: "Be of good cheer; I have overcome the world" (John 16:33). The world He has overcome includes all of our temporal struggles and losses on this earth, most notably the emotional burdens that weigh us down from time to time. His glorious message is one of both eventual salvation and daily salvation—a divine rescue from daily pain and worry, as well as the voices of the world that indoctrinate us with a sense of shame and powerlessness.

In light of this promise from our God, we must learn how to lay our burdens on Christ in exchange for the gifts He offers—daily peace, love, mercy, encouragement, and hope, to name a few. Despite our latter-day heritage, without this application of the good news, we are as disadvantaged as our Samaritan sister at the ancient well. If we feel powerless before our own weaknesses, fears, and uncertainties of the future, we must come to comprehend Christ's declaration of identity and purpose more fully—for our divinity is tied to His.

Elder James E. Talmage teaches, "Woman [shall] be recompensed in rich measure for all [she] . . . has endured in mortality. Then shall woman reign by Divine right, a queen in the resplendent realm of her glorified state."[3] Perhaps this promised recompense can begin even now as we learn to access the gifts Christ offers us. To be restored, even "recompensed," by His living water, we need only come to understand and then embrace, as did our Samaritan sister, who He is and the power He commands on our behalf. "Whosoever drinketh of the water that I shall give . . . shall never thirst . . . [for there] shall be in [her] a well of water springing up into everlasting life" (John 4:14). By accepting His gifts with open arms, God's daughters can finally and ultimately take hold of this marvelous promise.

*Be of good cheer;
I have overcome
the world.*

THE *Gift* OF MERCY

But Jesus stooped down, and with his finger wrote on the ground,
as though he heard them not. . . .
And Jesus was left alone, and the woman standing in the midst.
—John 8:6, 9

In the story of the woman taken in adultery, we find a heartbreaking scene of cruelty and humiliation. In the scribes' and Pharisees' efforts to publicly disgrace her, they mercilessly drag this woman to her presumed execution. One can imagine both her shame and fear as she faces condemnation. Not only are these accusers indifferent toward the feelings and fate of their sister, but they also concern themselves with sin that they, having no authority from God, have no power to judge.

But Christ's mercy and wisdom overpower their ruthless judgment, and His response is breathtaking in its implications. When the woman's would-be executioners ask the Master if she should be stoned, He says unto them, "He that is without sin among you, let him first cast a stone at her" (John 8:7). Likely, a heavy silence would have filled the waiting crowd as Christ "stooped down, and wrote on the ground" (v. 8). And then the miracle.

"And they which heard it, being convicted by their own conscience, went out one by one, beginning at the eldest, even unto the last" (v. 9).

Although this might seem like the story's natural conclusion, the Apostle John feels there was more—something that, for us, is the central point.

There is something in many of us that particularly fails to forgive and forget earlier mistakes in life. . . . It is not good. It is not Christian. It stands in terrible opposition to the grandeur and majesty of the Atonement of Christ. To be tied to earlier mistakes is the worst kind of wallowing in the past from which we are called to cease and desist.

"And Jesus was left alone, and the woman standing in the midst" (v. 9). The implications of this detail are thought-provoking. Like our sister who was left alone, we stand in our daily courtrooms with no one but Christ. In spite of the many self-appointed juries in our mortal sphere who may heap harsh judgments upon us, we too are "left alone" with the only Judge who matters. And He is a merciful judge. He, our only legitimate accuser, does not condemn.

The accusers in that ancient temple crowd have their contemporaries today, whose scornful stares we must steadfastly ignore as we focus on

Christ. These "watchers" are anyone or anything that stands on the sidelines of our lives and draws our attention away from the hope He offers. And like these accusers of old, many today neither know us nor care about our feelings or fate. So why pay heed to them now, when, thankfully, these juries ultimately stand powerless?

As we begin to understand and accept the Master's endless gift of mercy, we drink from the well He spoke of "whose waters fail not" (Isaiah 58:11). Of course, as the Master gently reminds, we must "go, and sin no more" (John 8:11), but many times we harbor pain and injury long after we repent of the sin.

To truly accept Christ's gift of mercy, we must be disciples of that mercy—administering it not only to others but also to ourselves. Refusing this gift is to refuse the Atonement itself. As Elder Jeffrey R. Holland states, "There is something in many of us that particularly fails to forgive and forget earlier mistakes in life. . . . It is not good. It is not Christian. It stands in terrible opposition to the grandeur and majesty of the Atonement of Christ. To be tied to earlier mistakes is the worst kind of wallowing in the past from which we are called to cease and desist."[4]

Many of us indulge in painfully obsessing over past or present weaknesses or the consequences born of such mistakes. But the disciple who accepts Christ's gift of mercy looks forward in faith to a resolution made possible through a power beyond her own. To have faith is to trust that the Atonement can repair whatever mistakes we have made by carving new blessings and opportunities out of broken things.

Elder Robert D. Hales assures us that nothing is beyond the scope of the Atonement. Christ has not just saved us from eternal condemnation, but His reach covers our immediate condemnation as well. Elder Hales explains, "Let me assure you that your situa-

Through Him, every struggle can be for our experience and our good.

The future is as bright as your faith.

tion is not beyond the reach of our Savior. Our challenges, including those we created by our own decisions, are part of our test in mortality. Through Him, every struggle can be for our experience and our good (see D&C 122:7)."[5]

We can experience great peace in knowing that even the challenges we create for ourselves, whether through ignorance, lack of experience, or irresponsibility, can be resolved—on this earth—for our benefit. Even serious sins do not condemn us to a broken future if we appropriately repent. President Boyd K. Packer has unequivocally declared: "There is no habit, no addiction, no rebellion, no transgression, no offense exempted from the promise of complete forgiveness. . . . Restoring what *you cannot restore*, healing the wound *you cannot heal*, fixing that which *you* broke and *you* cannot fix is the very purpose of the Atonement of Christ."[6]

The Savior can and will fix everything if we will turn to Him with full purpose of heart and accept His gift of mercy, waiting in faith for His time of action. He has promised He will not leave us to any malevolent crowd or to stumble alone under the consequences of our choices. He has prepared a way for His repentant daughters to humbly make their way through the crowd to safety: "I am the light of the world: he that followeth me shall not walk in darkness, but shall have the light of life" (John 8:12). Our mistakes must not destroy our futures. We will not have to walk in darkness; as Isaiah promises, "Who is among you that feareth the Lord, that obeyeth the voice of his servant, that walketh in darkness, and hath no light? let him trust in the name of the Lord, and stay upon his God" (Isaiah 50:10). President Monson adds his own testimony to Isaiah's, reinforcing the eternal nature of this glorious promise: "The future is as bright as your faith."[7]

We are in the process of perfection. It was not meant to be a single event. If this awareness of our imperfections leads to depression or discouragement, we must rally to the gift of mercy, knowing that despair is not of God. "That which

When we allow ourselves to feel 'encircled about eternally in the arms of his love,' we feel safe.

doth not edify is not of God" (D&C 50:23). The Savior's will is always to build us up, not tear us down. Let us consider our emotions; after assuring we have done all that's possible to repair our mistakes, we can examine our feelings and thoughts: are they uplifting, edifying? If not, then they are not of God, and we can—in good conscience—dismiss them from our minds.

Sister Bonnie D. Parkin, former Relief Society general president, asks, "Do we frequently reject the Lord's love that He pours out upon us in much more abundance than we are willing to receive? Do we think we have to be perfect in order to deserve His love? When we allow ourselves to feel 'encircled about eternally in the arms of his love' (2 Nephi 1:15), we feel safe, and we realize that we don't need to be immediately perfect."[8]

The gift that allows us the process of perfection—the process of messing up, learning, and becoming better—is the mercy of Christ. As with our forgiven sister in ancient times, we can joyfully accept the gift He died to give us, knowing that even as the crowd of accusers seems to grow thick about us, He—the supreme Judge—asks us, "*Woman, where are . . . thine accusers?*" (John 8:10, emphasis added). For in our daily efforts toward eventual perfection, there is none authorized to stand there but Him. In judgment, we stand before the One who came "not . . . to condemn the world; but that the world through him might be saved" (John 3:17).

THE *Gift* OF EXPERIENCE

I am the resurrection, and the life: he that believeth in me,

though he were dead, yet shall he live:

And whosoever liveth and believeth in me shall never die.

Believest thou this?

— John 11:25–26

Before Mary and Martha endure the loss of their beloved brother, we are reassured unequivocally that "Jesus loved Martha, and her sister, and Lazarus" (John 11:5). This detail is key, for only in the glow of that declaration can we understand the Savior's deliberate orchestration of their unique and briefly painful experience. Otherwise, we might wonder how He could possibly delay His return and allow His friends to face suffering and death alone.

Upon His arrival in the hilly outskirts of Bethany, Jesus' compassion permanently sets the record straight. For "when Mary . . . fell down at his feet . . . [and He] therefore saw her weeping," as well as when he saw where Lazarus was laid, "Jesus wept" (v. 32–33, 35).

Here the stage is set for the Redeemer to perform a miracle that would testify of His divinity to all present, but we find that He cares equally for the tender feelings of those He will intimately tutor through the process. In fact, this experience is clearly engineered not only to help the masses come to know Christ but to allow Mary and Martha—through their suffering—to know their Savior even more thoroughly. And as painful as is Lazarus's death, this gift of experience opens a door to a knowledge of the omnipotence and role of their Savior that they can internalize in no other way.

The price we paid to become acquainted with God was a privilege to pay.

We see this personalized lesson materialize as Jesus approaches Lazarus's grave; He is not engaged in public speechmaking before this impending miracle but is instead found in private conversation with Martha. It is her understanding of His power and purposes that seems to concern Him most. "Said Martha unto Jesus, Lord, if thou hadst been here, my brother had not died" (John 11:21). Christ then gently comforts, "Thy brother shall rise again" (v. 23). This suffering sister likely responds through choked tears, but with faith in that eventual promise, she answers, "I know that he shall rise again in the resurrection at the last day" (v. 24).

Seeing that she does not fully understand His message, the Master clarifies that the new life He offers is not limited to the physical nor the future resurrection: "I am the resurrection, and the life: he that believeth in me, though he were dead, yet shall he live: And whosoever liveth and believeth in me shall never die. Believest thou this?" (v. 25–26).

Christ is asking more than whether she believes in His teachings or His title. Martha's tearful testimony of Christ is admirably loyal yet still incomplete. Christ's promise of life does not concern Lazarus alone but also Martha herself. Her ability to live abundantly amid loss, to

access the power of peace and hope the Savior offers, is at stake. She may grasp her Lord's oft-stated promise of peace but seemingly only regarding its future implications—she understands that her brother will someday live again but not that the Master has the ability to validate that offer now. Martha has just been given the secret to eternal life, the grand secret of the ages.

Her sister, Mary, seems to equally misunderstand Christ's limitless power, for when she sees Christ, "she [falls] down at his feet, [also] saying unto him, Lord, if thou hadst been here, my brother had not died" (v. 32), emphasizing that the Master has come too late to rescue Lazarus.

Martha and Mary's humble yet temporal vision limits their access to the mysteries of God. As Jesus reminds them, "Said I not unto thee, that, if thou wouldest believe, thou shouldest see the glory of God?" (v. 40) He is now teaching of His broader mission—to provide hope, even after all logical hope seems lost. With the removal of the stone that seals Lazarus's tomb, Christ also removes any limitations these sisters would naively put on His power to redeem. The particular gift they wish for and receive—that Lazarus would not have died—was not the gift that will bless them most. The gift that will lead to a better understanding of their God is yet to come.

When the painful lessons of loss, failure, or an uncertain future come to us, it is a sign of the Master's faith in us—in our ability to withstand the leveling experiences that, paradoxically, draw us nearer to Him. As Wayne Brickey points out, "Oddly enough, our vision sometimes improves when our conditions worsen, creating an occasional windowpane, or window of pain, in the veil. A paralyzing problem can bring the stillness that causes us to pause, and, for a change, reverently look at the whole scene, which is the smallest scene we can trust."[9]

Christ's faith in Mary and Martha's ability to see through the veil is evident when He "abode two days still in the same place" after hearing of Lazarus's illness and knowing His friend would

Oddly enough, our vision sometimes improves when our conditions worsen, creating an occasional windowpane, or window of pain, in the veil. A paralyzing problem can bring the stillness that causes us to pause, and, for a change, reverently look at the whole scene, which is the smallest scene we can trust.

die (v. 6). He says to His confused disciples, "I am glad *for your sakes* that I was not there, to the intent ye may believe" (v. 15; emphasis added).

Perhaps, oddly, the required exchange for the gift of Christ's faith in and love for us can be exacting, but it is one that both God and we will find redemptive in the end. In speaking of this cost, one survivor of the brutal Martin Handcart experience reveals, "Everyone of us came through [that experience] with the absolute knowledge that God lives, for we became acquainted with Him in our extremities! . . . Was I sorry that I chose to come by handcart? No. Neither then nor any minute of my life since. The price we paid to become acquainted with God was a privilege to pay."[10]

Sometimes God calms the storm, and sometimes He lets the storm rage and calms His child.

The greater gift that Christ offers Mary and Martha is the gift of experience: to endure a trial until they come to know who He is and how His power can impact and dispel every moment of their fear or suffering. He offers the same today. As with all of His gifts, the endowment of experience brings peace—and yet "not as the world giveth" (John 14:27), for its bestowal does not require that our particular trials be taken away. In permitting these trials—in spite of His power to eliminate them—He allows a greater understanding of the divine purposes of God and personal refinement to emerge.

In our moments of pain, may we remember what Elder Jeffrey R. Holland teaches:

To those who stagger or stumble, He is there to steady and strengthen us. In the end He is there to save us, and for all this He gave His life. However dim our days may seem they have been darker for the Savior of the world.

In fact, in a resurrected, otherwise perfected body, our Lord of this sacrament table has chosen to retain for the benefit of His disciples the wounds in His hands and His feet and His side—signs, if you will, that painful things happen even to the pure and perfect. Signs, if you will, that pain in this world is not evidence that God doesn't love you. It is the wounded Christ who is the captain of our soul—He who yet bears the scars of sacrifice, the lesions of love and humility and forgiveness.[11]

May we take great comfort, as did Mary and Martha during perhaps the greatest trial of their lives, in the truth that "sometimes God calms the storm, and sometimes He lets the storm rage and calms His child."[12] The former brings us to understand merely His power over the elements; the latter brings us to know the One who has all power to save our souls.

May we take great comfort . . .

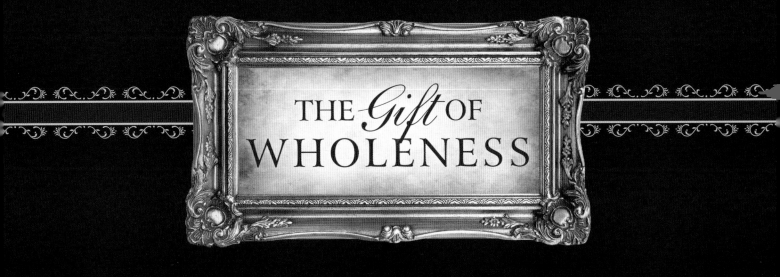

THE *Gift* OF WHOLENESS

And he said unto her, Daughter,
be of good comfort: thy faith hath made thee whole.
—LUKE 8:48

In ancient Israel, the "issue of blood" was considered unclean, whether during a woman's menses or on the occasion of childbirth. This sets the stage for the challenges facing a tender daughter of God who suffers the continuous issue of blood day after day and year after year. In Luke 8, we learn precious details about this woman who copes with her trial for twelve long years, a seemingly insurmountable hardship. Her desperation is so great that she "spent all of her living upon physicians" (Luke 8:43).

She seeks the care of the medical healers but to no avail. They have no answers for her condition, which means that, in essence, she is an outcast according to societal norms of her day. And for twelve years, she is considered unclean. According to Jewish tradition, she is not only "impure herself; she also contaminates others, even those in her proximity."[13] It's anyone's guess what has happened to her family, whether she has a husband or children from whom she has to separate herself. A hint in the text that she spends "*her* living" tells us that she may have been given a stipend, but she is apparently not under the care of a husband or any other family members (v. 43; emphasis added).

It's amazing to think that she spends twelve years in this limiting and isolating condition. And at the end of those years, her funds are depleted and her options are gone. She is left in

Yet, we must remember that it is the seed of faith that pulled her through, that comforted her, and enabled her to endure this twelve-year trial. Our faith in the Lord becomes paramount when we come to understand that He will eventually heal all wounds and that as we "endure to the end [we] shall have eternal life."

her deplorable condition to suffer through the days and nights alone, with no hope of being healed through the medicinal knowledge of her time.

Yet, she has faith. This is remarkable to consider. Twelve years of ill health and desperation could easily lead to failed hope. Where does her valiant faith come from? How can she, after so long, believe she could be made whole by simply touching the Savior's garment when every professional has failed to heal her?

Her prayers must be fervent, even desperate at times. She has a glimmer of faith that will soon radiate into something much more grand. We may wonder what goes through her mind as she hears stories of Jesus' ministry.

At this time, Jesus is well on His path of healing and teaching. He has performed many miracles already, and stories of these miracles surely precede His arrival in any town or village. This is made evident when Jesus follows Jairus to see his dying twelve-year-old daughter; everywhere the Savior "went the people thronged him" (Luke 8:42).

Jesus' growing reputation stirs up a desire in the people to be around Him. To be blessed by Him. To be healed by Him. Likely, the woman with the issue of blood hears of Jesus healing the centurion's servant (Luke 7:10), raising the son of the widow Nain from the dead (v. 15), and calming the tempest-tossed sea (Luke 8:24). Or perhaps she hears of other miracles, but certainly, she senses who this Man is and what He is capable of.

Matthew tells us that she "said within herself, If I may but touch his garment, I shall be whole" (Matthew 9:21). Given her perpetual "uncleanness," does the question, "Am I worthy of this blessing?" cross her mind? We may never know, but we do know she tries to hide after touching Jesus' garment. Perhaps she is afraid, or perhaps she is just so used to people avoiding her and so used to living in the shadows that she doesn't want to be seen by anyone, especially Jesus. When He stops, He insists He's felt power leave Him, power that heals: "I perceive that *virtue* is gone out of me" (Luke 8:46; emphasis added). The word *virtue* comes from a Greek term meaning "force, power, abundance, or strength," which rounds out the meaning of the "virtue" that leaves Christ and enters the woman.

Interestingly enough, "straightway" her issue of blood is "dried up; and she felt in *her* body that she was healed of that plague" (Mark 5:29). The twelve years

If I may but touch his garment, I shall be whole.

Thy faith hath made thee whole;

go in peace.

of misery has miraculously and vividly come to an end.

As Jesus pauses in the crowd to look for her, the woman slips out of hiding and "[comes] trembling, and falling down before him" (Luke 8:47) to confess or to bear testimony that it is she who had touched His robe and that she had been healed immediately.

When she explains this to Jesus, He replies, "Daughter, be of *good comfort*: thy faith hath made thee whole; go in peace" (v. 48; emphasis added). "Good comfort" also refers to "courage" in the Greek root. Since we don't know if our trials will last for twelve days or twelve years or perhaps even a lifetime, Christ's words "be of good comfort" bring us an added insight during the times we face challenges. The Savior's gift of wholeness can give us courage to endure in the event that our trial is long-term.

Almost simultaneous to the moment of the woman's confession, Jesus receives the news that Jairus's twelve-year-old daughter has died. His response to the messenger: "Fear not: believe only, and she shall be made whole" (v. 50). Jesus then proceeds to the young girl's home, and, in another miracle, raises her from her deathbed.

In a short space of time, Christ heals two women: one, a twelve-year-old girl on the cusp of womanhood; and the other, a woman who has been suffering in equal years to Jairus's daughter's entire life. These two miracles are only a couple of such that the Savior performed then and still performs today.

The Savior's power to heal the issue of blood and make the woman "whole" didn't stop when her physical blood issue ceased but likely included purification as well. Since blood was considered unclean during this ancient era, cleansing rituals were an important part of washing away the impurity, whether it was for a woman with an issue of blood or for a new mother who had just given birth. The blood associated with menses or childbirth is only considered a "physical impurity" that requires the purification sacrifice at the altar, though the woman has "committed no moral wrong that requires divine forgiveness."[14]

Fear not: believe only, and she shall be made whole.

In this vein, it might be plausible to assume the woman with the issue of blood is required to undergo a cleansing ritual or offer a purification sacrifice. Regardless, through Jesus' statement, telling her that she has been made whole and that she can "go in peace," He has given her a clean report of health. Similarly, through the blood sacrifice of the Atonement, we are given a clean report of health, emotionally and spiritually, as we turn to the Master healer and allow His words "go in peace" to enter our hearts.

In addition to clean health, the Savior gives the woman reentrance to her former life—a life with friends and family, a life in which she can now worship at the temple, a life where she becomes a part of society again. No longer the lone, suffering woman, her faith has increased and has healed her in more ways than one. Yet, we must remember that it is the seed of faith that pulled her through, that comforted her, and enabled her to endure this twelve-year trial. Our faith in the Lord becomes paramount when we come to understand that He will eventually heal all wounds and that as we "endure to the end [we] shall have eternal life" (D&C 14:7).

We learn in D&C 46:19 that one of the gifts of the Spirit is "to have faith to be healed." The woman with the issue of blood had this gift. Did she have the gift of faith to be healed all along? Yes. When Jesus comes to her town, she takes the opportunity to act on that gift in its fullness. We, too, can act on this same gift

The Savior has power enough to heal us all in each and every aspect of our lives, if we but reach out to Him.

and have faith that healing will come through the Savior.

Many of us have corners of our past that may not be healed yet. We may face physical hardships, such as the woman in Luke 8, or we may suffer emotional, mental, or spiritual bereftness, leaving us without a sense of wholeness. Some of our trials may last much longer than twelve years, perhaps even a lifetime. And when we are in the midst of our trials, we might feel discouragement and wonder when our challenge will be eased or lifted. The time frame of our trial may continue longer than we like, despite our prayers and fasting. We might think that our pleas are left unheard.

We must understand that the Lord has His own timetable, and we must trust that the infinite healing will come and our trial will be lifted: "Ye receive your reward; yea, ye shall have mercy restored unto you again; ye shall have justice restored unto you again; ye shall have a righteous judgment restored unto you again; and ye shall have good rewarded unto you again" (Alma 41:14). Let us not forget that while we are waiting for that complete and total healing, the Lord has power to strengthen us so we can "bear up [our] burdens with ease" (Mosiah 24:15).

Even from the beginning of life, we do not come to earth whole. We go through many developmental changes as infants in order to talk and walk. More changes occur as we age and experience young adulthood. As women, we go through another round of changes if we bear children. But still, we are not whole. And we cannot become whole by ourselves. Only the Savior came to earth as a whole being, and only through Him can we fill our missing parts and become cleansed or purified and go forward "in peace," as He bade our sister long ago.

We can embrace the gift of wholeness and become whole as the Savior is whole. Although we most likely won't find ourselves in a crowded marketplace where we are presented with the opportunity to reach out and touch the hem of the Savior's robe, we can find other ways to accept the Savior's gift to us. Sometimes events in our lives keep us from feeling whole, or other challenges keep us from feeling worthy enough to partake of spiritual gifts, but there is good news for all of us.

In D&C 59:8, we learn how we can embrace the gifts available from the Savior: "Thou shalt offer a sacrifice unto the Lord thy God in righteousness, even that of a broken heart and a contrite spirit." Truman Madsen says a "broken [heart] now does not mean distressed or tormented, it means an open heart. It means, as one of our brethren has taught us, a heart that is susceptible to the spirit and willing to keep His covenants. A broken heart is an open heart and He can fill it."[15]

As we bring our open hearts to the Savior, to the altar of His Atonement, we can receive His radiant wholeness. Each Sabbath day, we are invited to partake of the Savior's magnificent offering to us. The sacrament bread and water represent His wholeness, His gift, and His virtue.

The sacrament is a weekly reminder that we can proceed with great comfort and put our faith in Joseph Smith's stunning statement: "All your losses will be made up to you in the resurrection, provided you continue faithful. By the vision of the Almighty I have seen it."[16]

If we partake of the holy sacrament with an open heart, the extraordinary gift of wholeness will be ours for the taking. By embracing one

[A] broken [heart] now does not mean distressed or tormented, it means an open heart. It means, as one of our brethren has taught us, a heart that is susceptible to the spirit and willing to keep His covenants. A broken heart is an open heart and He can fill it.

gift, we are then able to embrace the next, as is made clear in this illuminating passage: "For unto him that receiveth it shall be given more abundantly, even power" (D&C 71:6).

The gift of wholeness is available to each of us, no matter how broken we might feel. The Savior has power enough to heal us all in each and every aspect of our lives, if we but reach out to Him, fully partake of His virtue, and step through the open door of His offered salvation.

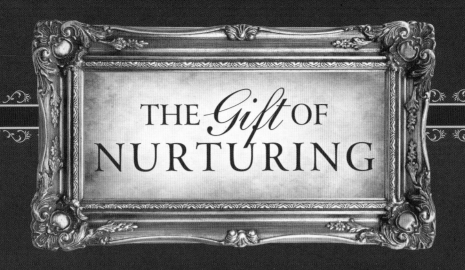

THE *Gift* OF NURTURING

For with God nothing shall be impossible.

—Luke 1:37

Remarkably, a woman "first received a divine testimony about the coming of the Messiah."[17] That woman is Elisabeth, cousin to the Virgin Mary. Although several prophecies about Mary lie within the scriptures and dozens of prophecies foretell the Savior's birth, Elisabeth is the first living witness (see Luke 1:42–43).

The reunion between the two cousins must be sweet. They live several days' travel apart, and the journey isn't easy. Elisabeth may have been surprised to receive a visit from her cousin, but it's clear that Mary sees Elisabeth as someone she can trust with a most important confession.

Like many women, Elisabeth is born with the innate ability and desire to nurture others. In "The Family: A Proclamation to the World," we are told, "Mothers are primarily responsible for the nurture of their children."

To nurture has long been thought of as a mother's role, but it is also a woman's role, regardless of whether she has earthly children. Relief Society General President Julie Beck explains that "helping growth occur through nurturing is truly a powerful and influential role bestowed on women."[18] This is a special gift the Savior offers to all women. It's reflected again and again through His example as He nurtures the women

Female roles did not begin on earth, and they do not end here. . . . In my experience I have seen that some of the truest mother hearts beat in the breasts of women who will not rear their own children in this life, but they know that "all things must come to pass in their time" and that they "are laying the foundation of a great work."

He encounters—reaching out His hand to raise the daughter of Jairus, comforting Mary and Martha after Lazarus's death, and stopping the crowd from casting stones at the woman taken in adultery. When we nurture others in our lives, just as the Savior does, we draw closer to Him because we come to understand His motives and His love for us and for those around us. We learn to see others as He sees them, and we long to bestow on them the same love He bestows.

A true test of nurturing appears on Elisabeth's doorstep in the form of her young, unmarried, pregnant cousin. Elisabeth knows about unexpected pregnancies. She, herself, has been barren most of her life. Yet, well past the child-bearing years, Elisabeth's husband, Zacharias, is visited by the angel Gabriel, who proclaims, "Fear not, Zacharias: for thy prayer is heard; and thy wife Elisabeth shall bear thee a son, and thou shalt call his name John" (Luke 1:13).

Although Elisabeth's conception is much different from Mary's, both are miraculous and both are foretold by the prophets. Elisabeth's son's birth is declared before he is even conceived, just as the angel prophesies to Mary about her son (Luke 1:13–17).

Once the two women realize the miracle of both conceptions, it must forge an even stronger bond between them. Elisabeth's son, John, will eventually pave the way for Mary's son, Jesus, and Elisabeth herself paves the way for Mary by welcoming her into her home. This allows Mary, in turn, to serve Elisabeth, demonstrating how acts of service benefit giver as much as receiver.

As detailed in Luke, when the first interaction takes place between Elisabeth and Mary, we learn a great deal about Elisabeth's gift of nurturing. She demonstrates pure joy in having Mary stay with her and holds no envy for her privileged cousin—a cousin who has been honored as the mother of the Savior.[19] She even goes so far as to testify with a surety, "Blessed *art* thou among women, and blessed *is* the fruit of thy womb" (Luke 1:42). Elisabeth's spiritual strength shines when she recognizes Mary as "the mother of [her] Lord" (Luke 1:43).

It appears that by visiting Elisabeth, Mary is led to the one person—Elisabeth—whom God has prepared to guide Mary through the fears and questions she surely experiences during those first weeks following the angel's announcement. Plainly, because Elisabeth has embraced and developed her gift of nurturing, she is prepared to bestow her love on her cousin.   Elisabeth's

Blessed art thou among women, and blessed is the fruit of thy womb.

ability to love instead of judge unrighteously creates an atmosphere in which Mary and her unborn Child can thrive; whereas if Elisabeth had not been nurturing, Mary may have been left to the devises of the world and faced even greater challenges with the incredible role she had been given.

Just as Elisabeth nurtures Mary, so does Jesus become the One to nurture all women. Elisabeth's warm embrace and welcoming words toward her cousin reflect the marvelous gift the Savior offers us all. The Savior extends His loving arms, and He tenderly invites us to come unto Him. Yet first, we must find a way to arrive at His doorstep.

In order to make it to the Savior's doorstep, we must prepare and practice. As women, we have been given the privileged gift of nurturing. The greatest example of how to accept and use our gift of nurturing is found in the Master of us all.

But what if we don't have children or aren't in a teaching position? Can we still use our gift of nurturing to bless those around us and in return bless ourselves? Absolutely. A woman's intrinsic

character is to nurture, just as Christ nurtures. In this light, Isaiah reminds barren women, "Break forth into singing, and cry aloud, thou *that* didst not travail with child: for more *are* the children of the desolate than the children of the married wife, saith the Lord" (Isaiah 54:1). Sister Julie Beck echoes, "Female roles did not begin on earth, and they do not end here. . . . In my experience I have seen that some of the truest mother hearts beat in the breasts of women who will not rear their own children in this life, but they know that 'all things must come to pass in their time' and that they 'are laying the foundation of a great work' (D&C 64:32–33)."[20]

Like Elisabeth, we may be given the opportunity to nurture a cousin, a ward sister we visit teach, or some other person in need. Let us consider if we are prepared to open our door and meet the needs of the person standing on our figurative doorstep. Have we, like Elisabeth, filled our vessels with the light of Christ so that we may, when needed, be that one person?

Just as we fill our vessels in order to share with others, doing so, in turn, fills our lives with light. We become the light-filled vessels others

The Savior extends His loving arms,
and He tenderly invites us to come unto Him.

25

For my yoke is easy, and my burden is light.

seek when we embrace His gift of nurturing. This gift is one to be both cherished and developed. The gifts of the Spirit are not meant to add burdens to our already pressing lives. They are meant to strengthen us and teach us how to become more like the Savior. There may be times in our lives when we find ourselves carrying too much of a load. Elder Neal A. Maxwell says, "May I speak . . . to those who carry their own load and more . . . who, though laboring devotedly in the Kingdom, have recurring feelings of falling forever short. . . . There is a difference . . . between being 'anxiously engaged' and being over-anxious and thus underengaged."[21]

We may struggle with a variety of trials, including ones that seem too large to manage on our own or trials that run for an extended period of time. We may wonder how we can cope when our trials become so overwhelming that we don't know what to focus on first. Or we may not know how to endure when there seems to be no end in sight. In D&C 88:119, we are counseled to "prepare every needful thing." Couple that with the words found in Luke 10:42, "But one thing is needful: and Mary hath chosen that good part." We must nourish ourselves, just as Mary does and just as Elisabeth does. We must sit at the Savior's feet and listen to His words. By doing this, we can put our faith in the one true gospel, even in the midst of many trials, by

focusing on the Savior and establishing a "house of prayer, a house of fasting, a house of faith, a house of learning, a house of glory, a house of order, a house of God" (D&C 88:119).

When a burden is too large to bear ourselves and we feel "heavy laden," we must remember that there is Someone who is waiting to share it and, if necessary, take the burden from us. The Lord has invited us: "Come unto me" (Matthew 11:28). With these simple words, *come unto me*, the Lord is offering to nurture us. Just as our nurturing gives others "rest," the Lord will give us rest.

At times, when we feel overwhelmed by pressures to meet everyone's needs around us, we can find tender comfort and sweet relief when we take the Savior's yoke upon us (see Matthew 11:29). He has given us this glowing promise: "For my yoke *is* easy, and my burden is light" (v. 30). He provides us a clear way, and offers us exceptional spiritual gifts so we can achieve the most important goal—returning to live with Him.

We can pray and ponder about these wonderful gifts, and by so doing, we allow Him into our hearts and are able to embrace the nurturing He offers us. Let's put faith in these words spoken about His daughter Elisabeth: "For with God nothing shall be impossible" (Luke 1:37). As women, we are frequently the caretakers, the bringers of charity, and the providers of comfort. And we must not forget that, in turn, He will remember us and He will take care of us.

Truman Madsen shares these beautiful words, "Sisters, in His sacrament, the Lord gives us glimpses of ourselves. And in self-examination we are most blessed when we see ourselves as we are seen by Him. . . . In this world, we do not really grasp who we are until we know *whose* we are. And week after week the Master invites us to take upon us His name so that we will never forget whose we are."[22]

The examples that Mary and Elisabeth set for us before and during Christ's life are spread before us in the holy scriptures and give us a glimpse of how they, in their own unique way,

rely on the Savior. Their lives are filled with grave challenges, some that are heartbreaking, yet they embrace each other at their first meeting and offer each other support and pure love. They transcend the seemingly impossible by embracing the Lord's amazing gifts.

Elisabeth is prepared to nurture the mother of the Lord. As she develops her gift of nurturing, she is, in turn, nurtured by the Spirit. Likewise, as we use our divine gift of nurturing others, we will find ourselves lovingly nurtured by the Savior, enabling us to achieve our divine potential and giving us the understanding that "with God nothing shall be impossible." We will reap resplendent rewards in the hereafter.

THE *Gift* OF SEEING

*Jesus saith unto her, Woman, why weepest thou?
whom seekest thou? . . . [Then] Jesus saith unto her, Mary.
She turned herself, and saith unto him,
Rabboni; which is to say, Master.*

—JOHN 20:15–16

Mary Magdalene witnesses the first sign of the Resurrection in the eastern hemisphere. On that Sunday morning, three days after Christ's Crucifixion, she hurries to His burial place, arriving before the rosy dawn when the sky is "yet dark" (John 20:1). There, Mary "*seeth* the stone [has been] taken away from the sepulchre" (v. 1; emphasis added).

She does not know Christ has risen but thinks His tomb has been robbed. Her Savior has died, and there is no longer a body to which she can pay respect. Just like today, in the ancient world, it was important for survivors to visit the burial place of their loved ones in order to honor that person's life. The robbing of the tomb had robbed Mary of the only service she could still render Him.

No doubt it is with great distress and apprehension that Mary runs to find Simon Peter and John to tell them the news. They come to examine the empty tomb, and as described by Mary, only the burial linen remains inside. The body is missing. The disciples can do nothing. And though they eventually leave, Mary cannot yet bear to leave Christ's last known physical location, so she remains, weeping.

As she bends down to inspect the tomb again, she *looked* and witnesses another sign of the Resurrection: she "seeth two angels in white

As we focus on other concerns in our lives, we may miss seeing the Savior standing right beside us. Mary Magdalene is so focused on the Savior's missing body that she doesn't consider that He might be resurrected.

sitting, the one at the head, and the other at the feet, where the body of Jesus had lain" (v. 12). Another instance of seeing, and yet, she still does not truly see in a spiritual sense.

When Mary turns, she "[sees] Jesus standing" but does not realize it is Him (v. 14). How can this be? How can she see the glorified Savior and not know it is Him? He stands right in front of her, yet she does not recognize Him.

Many of us have representations of the Savior in our homes, as well as His words in scripture throughout our houses, but like the troubled Mary, we sometimes do not truly see Him. As we focus on other concerns in our lives, we may miss seeing the Savior standing right beside us. Mary Magdalene is so focused on the Savior's missing body that she doesn't consider that He might be resurrected.

Only when the Savior calls her by name is she able to see Him.

The Savior calls our names. Are we listening? Sometimes we find ourselves too caught up in our ever-busy lives to see Him and embrace the gifts He offers. When we are stressed, worried, overwhelmed, or even filled with self-recrimination, this is the time to include Him in our lives and take comfort in His love for us.

Regardless of whether we are in our modern-day homes, looking at pictures of the Savior, or standing in front of the empty tomb, we have a divine invitation to come—to see who the Savior is. And when we at last see Him in all His glory and magnificence, we can finally understand how He sees us.

We can better appreciate how Christ sees us when we consider how we view the children in our lives. Whether or not we are physical mothers on earth, we are teachers, neighbors, and caregivers of these precious children. In them, we see their vast potential. The children may not see it for themselves; in fact, they may deny their gifts and talents when we point them out. We can try to convince them until we run out of words, but only when they allow their minds to open and embrace new possibilities can they understand, or see, the potential that lies within.

At a celebrated time in history, Mary Magdalene's tears prevent her from truly "seeing." Because of her emotional state, she is not able to open her mind to a new possibility of what the Savior might be doing or how He might appear. Only when she dries her tears and casts away her other concerns and preoccupations is she able to see His resurrected body. Elder Richard G. Scott reminds us, "The inspiring influence of the Holy Spirit can be overcome or masked by strong emotions, such as anger, hate, passion, fear, or pride. When such influences are present . . . [these] strong emotions overcome the delicate promptings of the Holy Spirit."[23]

We would do well to slow down a little . . . and truly see the things that matter most.

The Savior needs to become our anchor.

If we overcome emotions that tear us down and dim our perception of the future, we will see our Savior's loving gaze and understand His marvelous plans. Imagine the potential the Savior sees in us. Like a woman seeing the potential in children that surround her, the Savior has the same eternal perspective about us. He understands us. He knows us. He sees us. He is there, standing beside us, calling us by name.

With all the surrounding distractions of life, the Savior needs to become our anchor. We must be willing to put time and effort into what matters most. President Dieter F. Uchtdorf says, "We would do well to slow down a little, proceed at the optimum speed for our circumstances, focus on the significant, lift up our eyes, and *truly see the things that matter most.*"[24]

In the spirit of invitation, let us push aside the obstacles that prevent us from truly seeing our Savior. Let us "see that all these things are done in wisdom and order; for it is not requisite that a man should run faster than he has strength" (Mosiah 4:27). Let us pause and ponder on the luminous words of scripture. Look beyond the Mary Magdalene concerns—of the physical and temporal around us—and look into the heart of the Savior, where we can see and feel the pure and absolute love He has for each of us.

After Christ speaks to Mary, she recognizes Him at last, in all of His resurrected brilliance. Can we also look at the Savior and say, "Rabboni"—calling Him our "Master" (John 20:16)?

If we but allow the Savior to "wipe away all tears from [our] eyes" (Revelation 7:17), we can believe in His stunning promise of eternal life, where "there shall be no more death, neither sorrow, nor crying, neither shall there be any more pain: for the former things are passed away" (21:4). By understanding that He is real, that He is our Savior, and that we can see ourselves through His eyes, might we "bow the knee in praise now? Why not, by faith, cry a little less and see a little more—more clearly and more early—through the veil of tears?"[25]

If we use our gift of seeing to "see" the Savior now, we will understand that He has never left us alone on earth nor will He. Let us rejoice in this good news. His body is no longer in the tomb, allowing His love and care to continue to surround us. No matter what our challenges, He has not forgotten us, His precious sisters. He speaks directly to you and to me when He says with amazing compassion, "Yet will I not forget thee. Behold, I have graven thee upon the palms of *my* hands" (Isaiah 49:15–16).

We are never alone. We are loved by a kind-hearted Elder Brother, our gentle Savior, who holds us dear. Despite His grand mission of saving the innumerable souls throughout the eternities, Christ did not forget the needs of the one woman, even Mary Magdalene, at the site of the tomb. Likewise, He does not forget us in His infinite and matchless love. Nor will He ever.

Behold, I have graven thee upon the palms of my hands.

ENDNOTES

1 Ezra Taft Benson. "Do Not Despair," *Ensign*, November 1974, 65.

2 James Strong. *Strong's Exhaustive Concordance of the Bible*, entry 2098 Greek Index, Iowa Falls, IA: World Bible Publishers, 1986.

3 James E. Talmage. "The Eternity of Sex," *Young Woman's Journal*, October 1914, vol. 25.

4 Jeffrey R. Holland. "The Best Is Yet to Be," *Ensign*, January 2010, 22.

5 Robert D. Hales. "Becoming Provident Providers Temporally and Spiritually," *Ensign*, May 2009, 7.

6 Boyd K. Packer. "The Brilliant Morning of Forgiveness," *New Era*, April 2005, 4; emphasis added.

7 Thomas S. Monson. "Be of Good Cheer," *Ensign*, May 2009, 89.

8 Bonnie D. Parkin. "Eternally Encircled in His Love," *Ensign*, November 2006, 108.

9 Wayne E. Brickey. *Making Sense of Suffering*, Salt Lake City, UT: Deseret Book, 2001, 1.

10 David O. McKay. "Pioneer Women," *Relief Society Magazine*, January 1948, 8.

11 Jeffrey R. Holland. "This Do in Remembrance of Me," *Ensign*, November 1995, 69.

12 As quoted by David O. McKay. "Pioneer Women," *Relief Society Magazine*, January 1948, 8.

13 Jacob Milgrom. *The Anchor Bible: Leviticus 1–16: A New Translation with Introduction and Commentary*, New York: Doubleday, 1991, 763.

14 Jacob Milgrom. *The Anchor Bible: Leviticus 1–16: A New Translation with Introduction and Commentary*, New York: Doubleday, 1991, 760.

15 Truman Madsen. "The Savior, the Sacrament, and Self-Worth," BYU Women's Conference transcript, April 1999.

16 *Teachings of the Prophet Joseph Smith*, sel. Joseph Fielding Smith, 1976, Section Six 1843–44, 296.

17 S. Kent Brown. *Mary and Elisabeth*, American Fork, UT: Covenant Communications, 2002, 33.

18 Julie B. Beck. "Mothers Who Know," *Ensign*, November 2007, 76.

19 S. Kent Brown. *Mary and Elisabeth*, American Fork, UT: Covenant Communications, 2002, 28.

20 Julie B. Beck. "A 'Mother Heart,'" *Ensign*, May 2004, 75.

21 Neal A. Maxwell. "Notwithstanding My Weakness," *Ensign,* November 1976, 12.

22 Truman Madsen. "The Savior, the Sacrament, and Self-Worth," BYU Women's Conference transcript, April 1999; emphasis added.

23 Richard G. Scott. "To Acquire Spiritual Guidance," *Ensign*, November 2009, 6.

24 Dieter F. Uchtdorf. "Of Things That Matter Most," *Ensign*, November 2010, 19; emphasis added.

25 Wayne E. Brickey. *Making Sense of Suffering*, Salt Lake City, UT: Deseret Book, 2001, 135–36.

ART CREDITS

Page vi: *Light of the World* © 2011 Howard Lyon. For print information, go to www.fineart.howardlyon.com or call 480.241.7907.

Page viii: *For She Loved Much* © 2011 Simon Dewey. Courtesy of Altus Fine Art. For print information, go to www.altusfineart.com.

Page x: *Though Your Sins Be As Scarlet* © 2011 Howard Lyon. For print information, go to www.fineart.howardlyon.com or call 480.241.7907.

Page 2: *He Who Is Without Sin* © 2011 Liz Lemon Swindle. Used with permission from Foundation Arts. For print information, go to www.foundationarts.com or call 800.366.2781.

Page 3: *Jesus and the Woman Taken in Adultry* by Gustave Doré, *The Doré Bible Illustrations,* Dover Publications.

Page 4: *The Woman Taken in Adultry* by Harry Anderson © Pacific Press Publishing Association, Nampa, Idaho. Used by permission.

Page 6: *Raising of Lazarus* © Jeffrey Hein. For more information go to www.jeffreyhein.com/blog.

Page 9: *I Am the Resurrection* © 2011 Liz Lemon Swindle. Used with permission from Foundation Arts. For print information, go to www.foundationarts.com or call 800.366.2781.

Page 10: *Lazarus Raised from the Dead,* courtesy of *Treasury of Bible Illustrations Old and New Testament* by Julius Schnorr von Carolsfeld, Dover Publications.

Page 11: *Raising Lazarrus* by Carl Heinrich Bloch, courtesy of Det Nationalhistoriske Museum på Frederiksborg, Hillerød.

Page 12: *Trust in the Lord* © 2011 Liz Lemon Swindle. Used with permission from Foundation Arts. For print information, go to www.foundationarts.com or call 800.366.2781.

Page 14: *Touch of Faith* © 2011 Simon Dewey. Courtesy of Altus Fine Art. For print information, go to www.altusfineart.com.

Page 15: *Faith Has Made You Well,* courtesy of *The New Testament: A Pictorial Archive from Nineteenth-Century Sources.* Edited by Don Rice, Dover Publication.

Page 16: *Woman Touching the Hem of Christ's Robe* © Judith Mehr.

Page 19: Detail from *I Shall Be Whole* © 2009 Al R. Young. Courtesy of Al Young Studios. For print information, please visit www.alyoung.com.

Page 20: *Mary Kept All of These Things and Pondered Them In Her Heart* © 2011 Howard Lyon. For print information, go to www.fineart.howardlyon.com or call 480.241.7907.

Page 22: *Annunciation to Mary* © Joseph F. Brickey. For more information, go to www.josephbrickey.com.

Page 23: *Nativity* by Gustave Doré, *The Doré Bible Illustrations,* Dover Publications.

Page 24: *Refuge* © 2011 Liz Lemon Swindle. Used with permission from Foundation Arts. For print information, go to www.foundationarts.com or call 800.366.2781.

Page 25: *Mary's Visit to Elisabeth* by Carl Heinrich Bloch, courtesy of Det Nationalhistoriske Museum på Frederiksborg, Hillerød.

Page 27: *She Shall Bring Forth a Son* © 2011 Liz Lemon Swindle. Used with permission from Foundation Arts. For print information, go to www.foundationarts.com or call 800.366.2781.

Page 28: *Why Weepest Thou?* © 2011 Simon Dewey. Courtesy of Altus Fine Art. For print information, go to www.altusfineart.com.

Page 30: *Garden Tomb* by Jon McNaughton © McNaughton Fine Art Co. For print information, go to www.mcnaughtonart.com.

Page 31: *The Resurrection* by Gustave Doré, *The Doré Bible Illustrations,* Dover Publications.

Page 32: *Why Weepest Thou?* © 2011 Liz Lemon Swindle. Used with permission from Foundation Arts. For print information, go to www.foundationarts.com or call 800.366.2781.